WATER

The Stuff of Life

PHILLIP DAY

GW00601967

Credence Publications

Water – The Stuff of Life

Copyright © 2004
Phillip Day

The right of Phillip Day to be identified as the Author of the Work has been asserted by him in accordance with the Copyright, Designs and Patents Act 1988.

First published in 2004
by Credence Publications

ISBN 1-904015-15-8

Manufactured in Great Britain by
Credence Publications
PO Box 3
TONBRIDGE
Kent TN12 9ZY UK
www.credence.org

1st ed.

Table of Contents

Introduction

'I know that most men, including those at ease with problems of the greatest complexity, can seldom accept even the simplest and most obvious truth if it would oblige them to admit the falsity of conclusions which they have delighted in explaining to colleagues, proudly taught to others, and which they have woven, thread by thread, into the fabric of their lives.' - **Leo Tolstoy**

'You medical people will have more lives to answer for in the other world than even we generals.' - **Napoleon Bonaparte**

'If you think you are healthy, you simply have not had enough tests yet.' – **Phillip Day**

Water is essential to life. Everyone knows it. From our youngest years when we first accepted that plants die without water, the singular importance of this most elemental ingredient to our own existence has been entrenched in the human psyche. A man cannot cross a desert without water. An astronaut cannot venture into space without water. A human may survive longer than a month and a half without solid foods to sustain him, but without water, he is dead within days.

The fact that water can heal the sick has been an ongoing wrangle in scientific circles for years. Not because there's any doubt about it, but because no-one wants to fund studies if the only thing they have to sell at the end of them are two atoms of hydrogen and one of oxygen. Ever since John Rockefeller and Abraham Flexner set up the modern medical system we know today and doctors became 'licensed' to prescribe and sell their chemicals, the nutrients of nature which daily sustain our bodies have been ignored in favour of the profitable chemical as the panacea for the ills of man. Even today, how your doctor is trained and what he has been taught to tell and prescribe you bears more relation to economics than what will actually heal. It is *sickness* which is Big Business. No-one's making much money out of *health* these days.

3

During the twenty years I have travelled the world reporting on health issues, interviewing doctors and writing numerous books and articles on the subject, I have become increasingly dismayed and angered at how knowledge of the simple has been systematically ignored in favour of the profitable. Back in the late 1970s, the revolution in healthcare was largely still in its infancy. Today, a significant percentage of the western populations have already learned to their chagrin the costly and tragic disaster that is pharmaceutical medicine. Millions hooked on benzodiazepine drugs. Millions killed with chemotherapy and radiation treatments for cancer. Millions of our precious children drugged up in the scientific belief they have 'behavioural disorders' only chemicals can solve. Got a headache, have a drug. Got a bad attitude, have a drug. If the only tool in your kit-box is a hammer, pretty soon everything starts looking like a nail.

The fact that lifestyle changes, living foods and fresh, clean water are in themselves largely the answer to our medical ills is complete nonsense to the technically-minded, university-trained MD. Even though it is common knowledge the human body becomes what it absorbs, most doctors are never taught nutrition. Even though everyone knows that food can change your mood (Valentine's Day depends on it), millions live enshrouded in the fog of the highly addictive 'anti-depressants' they have been told they cannot live without. Even though the human body comprises 70-73% water, your physician has been taught this water is nothing more than an inert solvent used to transport minerals, proteins, enzymes and other nutrients around the body. He has probably never heard the astonishing truth that water is far from inert, *that there is not one function or system in the body that is not controlled or regulated by the availability and distribution of water.*[1]

John Rockefeller's pharmaceutical industry today is a highly profitable legacy of death and betrayal, not just for the patient, but also for the trusting men and women who devoted their lives to helping others by becoming 'doctors'. Today, 70% of these same

---

[1] **Batmanghelidj, F**, *Water and Salt*, Tagman Press, 2003

4

men and women regret entering medicine. Why? They just don't see the majority of their efforts making people better.

The purpose of this overview booklet is to bring you the great news you will never hear from your doctor, his medical establishment, your 'healthcare provider' or your government. And that news is, **water heals.** But to appreciate why this tremendous boon to our health has been denigrated, vilified, ignored and even flat-out poisoned in favour of the constant tide of chemical nostrums, it serves us first to consider the disaster that has become 21st century healthcare in a little more detail. For only in understanding the catastrophic wrong-turns which have been taken at our expense in favour of the corporate balance sheet can the public ever hope to gain the full measure of the crimes which have been perpetrated against them.

Overly harsh?

Read on and be the judge.

Doctors – The Third Leading Cause of Death

Hard though it may be to accept at first, western healthcare has indeed become the third leading cause of death in most industrialised nations. In the Credence titles *Wake up to Health in the 21st Century* and *Health Wars*, author Steven Ransom and myself cover the harsh statistics plainly demonstrating that often doctors not only *don't* have the answer to what ails us, but instead do irreparable harm with those industry sanctioned 'cures' the public is bullied into accepting without question.

Medicine has made great strides in A & E trauma medicine and certain other areas, and, of course, doctors are not bad or evil people. But they have been trained in institutions funded by the drug industry, and so their licence to practise is dependent on them conforming to the medical orthodoxy of the day. Any use of treatments unsanctioned by the establishment can bring swift and summary retribution. No-one in Big Medicine is interested in natural treatments that cannot be patented and sold for great profit.

That doctors and their hospitals could, in themselves, be deadly to our health is rarely considered by the layman, whose respect for the unknowable, arcane secrets of doctors and their medicines borders on worship. Figures released in 1998 and published in *Environment and Health News* however make sobering reading:

'Australians may want to think twice before their next trip to the clinic. The chances of dying in hospital, or suffering some injury while there, stand at around 16% in Australia. Half this risk is due to doctor or hospital error – which means that 8% of hospital patients are accidentally killed or injured by the staff.' [2]

---

[2] *Environment and Health News*, Vol. 3, January 1998

In a recent emailed response to the *British Medical Journal* (BMJ), Ron Law, Executive Director of the NNFA in New Zealand and member of the New Zealand Ministry of Health Working Group advising on medical error, cites the following statistics and facts: Official Australian government reports reveal that preventable medical error in hospitals is responsible for 11% of all deaths in Australia,[3] [4] which is about 1 of every 9 deaths. *If deaths from properly researched, properly registered, properly prescribed and properly used drugs were added along with preventable deaths due to private practice it comes to a staggering 19%, which is almost 1 of every 5 deaths.*

New Zealand figures are very similar, according to Mr. Law. He states that the equivalent of New Zealand's second largest city (Christchurch) has been killed by preventable medical error and deaths from properly researched, properly registered, properly prescribed and properly used drugs in Australasia in the past decade and its biggest city Auckland either killed or permanently maimed.

Dr Joseph Mercola, who hosts the most comprehensive and frequently visited health research site on the Internet at www.mercola.com, has analysed Law's statistics:

'More than 5 million people have been killed by Western medical practice in the past decade (Europe, USA, Canada, Australia, and NZ) and 20 million killed or permanently maimed. Put another way, the economic impact of deaths due to preventable medical error and deaths from properly researched, properly registered, properly prescribed and properly used drugs is approximately $1 trillion over the past decade. Law notes that only 0.3% of these deaths are properly coded and classified in official statistics as being attributed to these causes.' [5]

---

3 **www.mercola.com** Iatrogenic Injury in Australia - This is the executive summary of a 150-page official report revealing 14,000 preventable medical error deaths (only in hospitals - not private practice). (Full report on Dr Mercola's file).

4 **Australian Bureau of Statistics** - Australian 1994 total deaths (1994) = 126,692, www.mercola.com, op. cit.

5 *British Medical Journal*, 11th November 2000; 321: 1178A (emailed response)

In July 2000, one of the world's most prestigious medical journals, *The Journal of the American Medical Association* (JAMA), reported that every year in the United States, 225,000 citizens are unnecessarily killed by western healthcare practices. JAMA's figures were later upgraded by the Nutrition Institute of America (NIA) to a more truthful 790,000, making the medical system in the US the leading cause of death in that country.[6] In Britain, this figure of iatrogenic (doctor-induced) death is reported in excess of 40,000, although the real toll, using the proper markers, is estimated to be not far short of 200,000. To put it into perspective for Britons, this is two and half times the capacity of an Olympic stadium, packed to the last seat, slaughtered EVERY YEAR by medical mishaps, incompetence and entrenched scientific error.

In the year 2000, my book *Health Wars* was published, documenting these crimes against humanity. These human rights atrocities are, if possible, more reprehensible given the fact that those culpable - the medical authorities, the media, the chemical/drug industry and government - know very well what they are doing, yet consistently lie, hedge, prevaricate and obfuscate to conceal the true extent of their part in this tragedy to protect their own financial agendas.

From the lies told about the safety of MMR through to the constant claims by cancer 'charities' that carcinogenic chemos and radiation are winning the war on cancer, the public of course remains both victim and paymaster. We are unsure who to believe, what to do or where to find impartial truth. We are stupefied we were talked into allowing our kids to be drugged up at school to make them more amenable. Fooled into allowing our elderly relatives to be drugged up in their care homes. Duped into giving our trust and savings to a drug-dealing cartel which presides over at least the third leading cause of death in society today if not the first two also (heart disease and cancer).

---

[6] www.campaignfortruth.com: Search on 'Death by Medicine'

Banking on fear

Concerning the alliance of Big Pharma, Big Government and Big Media, Steven Ransom writes:

'Using the mainstream media as their chosen vehicle for change, powerful vested interests within the pharmaceutical industry are deliberately instigating national and international fearsome headlines. Through these channels, the 'nightmare problem' – the epidemic – the psycho-plague, is manufactured. Take a look at these recent quotations and headlines as examples:

'Even if we rapidly eliminate SARS, we remain at risk of future viral mutations, and should expect more dangerous new viruses to emerge over the next ten years.' **Dr Patrick Dixon, April 2003**

PLAGUE ATTACK The horrifying spectre of terrorists turning themselves into walking biological weapons on Britain's streets was raised by doctors. Fanatics could be given smallpox and walk amongst us infecting people, yet we only have a vaccine for one in three. **Express Newspapers, 6th March 2003**

SMALLPOX KILLS! Smallpox kills about 30% of those infected with the disease. There is no cure, but there is a vaccine. If given before exposure, the vaccine will prevent the disease from appearing. But is there enough for everyone? **BBC NEWS, 13th January 2003**

FEARS OF KILLER FLU EPIDEMIC: The world is on the brink of a flu epidemic which could claim millions of lives. The mutant virus has already killed one man in Hong Kong. We need to find out as much as we can about this deadly new virus. **Express Newspapers, 21st February 2003**

TUBERCULOSIS! NEW SPECTRE OF THE WHITE DEATH - We had it beaten, but TB is back and deadlier than ever…. Anyone who refuses inoculation is a danger both to society and to himself. **Daily Mail, 30th March 2001**

MEASLES! Public health officials have stressed the severity of the situation. The Government is now urging parents to take heed of this warning and allow their children to be immunised with the MMR jab before an epidemic sweeps the nation. **Readers Digest, January 2001**

It is not hard to see what is going on here. Steven Ransom writes further:

'The crisis has now been firmly embedded into the minds of the populace. 'We must have a solution!' Lo and behold, a corporate solution is speedily proffered, usually in the form of vaccination, antibiotics and associated conventional 'ministrations'. The epidemic needing 'swift state intervention' has been nothing more than a Trojan Horse for creating immense profit for various pharmaceutical corporations. Throughout this whole process, we are being taught what to think about global health and disease, but not how.' [7]

Failing to heal

Traditional medicine has failed very conspicuously to halt the metabolic syndromes, such as heart disease, cancer and diabetes. It serves us to study the fundamental flaw in the basic methodology followed by allopathic[8] medicine today that is at the root of this devastation. The flaw is simply this: our medical peers are treating our bodies with toxic drugs, radical surgeries and poisonous radiation treatments to combat diseases that are, in almost all cases, either metabolic (nutritional) deficiency syndromes or diseases already caused by poisons (diseases of toxicity).

Doctors often do not appreciate the four major statements below that condemn their current treatment approaches to metabolic diseases:

---

7 **Ransom, Steven**, *Wake up to Health in the 21st Century*, Credence Publications 2003
8 allopathic – drug/technology based medicine, as practised by industrialised societies today

10

1. Metabolic diseases are the big killers (cancer, heart disease, etc.)
2. A metabolic disease is a disease that is wedded to your utilisation of food and its metabolism
3. No metabolic disease can be reversed by anything other than the missing metabolic preventative(s), which are always food factors
4. Doctors receive no formal training in nutrition

If we become what we absorb, and the body is the battlefield for the doctor, why *doesn't* our medical establishment train our doctors in nutrition – the most fundamental of body sciences? The long answer is, it's due to a complex web of greed, big business and ignorance.[9] The short answer is, fruits, veggies and cups of water don't make Porsche payments.

Teaching on nutrition

John Robbins cites statistics on western medical and nutritional curricula in his *Reclaiming our Health*:

➤ Number of accredited medical schools in the United States – 127
➤ Number with no required courses in nutrition - 95
➤ Average US physician's course work in nutrition during four years of medical school - 2.5 hours
➤ Percentage of first-year medical school students who consider nutrition to be important to their future careers - 74%
➤ Percentage who, after two years of medical school, still consider nutrition important - 13%
➤ Percentage of US physicians who are overweight - 55%
➤ Percentage of US physicians who eat the recommended daily servings of fruits and vegetables - 20% [10]

Dr M R C Greenwood, President of the American Society for Clinical Nutrition (ASCN), was responsible for the following article:

---

9 For a fuller investigation, see **Day, Phillip**, *Health Wars*, Credence 2001, www.credence.org
10 **Robbins, John**, *Reclaiming our Health*, Stillpoint Publ. 1987

Doctors Need More Nutrition Training: Nutrition experts say American physicians are under-trained when it comes to issues of nutrition and health. Less than 6% of medical school graduates receive adequate nutrition training. 'Until physicians are better trained to provide high levels of information on nutrition, Americans are missing countless opportunities to take advantage of the growing body of scientific research on the role of diet in preventing and treating disease.'[11]

Isn't it incredible that there should be any doubt whatsoever that food (which is essential to keep you alive and from which every cell in your body is formed) should in any way be doubted in its role in preventing and treating disease. Nutrition expert Dr Michael Klaper is the Director of the Institute of Nutritional Education and Research at Pompano Beach, Florida. He says:

'What's really tragic about this is that we were so busy learning how to fix broken arms, deliver babies and do all of those 'doctor' things in medical school that we considered nutrition to be boring. But after we get into practice, <u>we spend most of the day treating people with diseases that have huge nutritional concerns that have long been essentially ignored</u> [emphasis mine]. I frequently get calls from doctors across the country saying that their patients are asking questions about nutrition and its role in their conditions and they don't know what to tell them.'[12]

Steve Ransom writes in his Great News on Cancer: '*It appears that medical students begin with the best of intentions, but the pharmaceutically-oriented curriculum gradually reshapes their understanding. Another good barometer for measuring the importance the conventional medical community attaches to nutrition is by sampling hospital food. Budgetary restrictions aside, in a recent letter to the New England Journal of Medicine, a group of researchers contends that hospital food is not healthy. Led by Dr Adam Singer of the State University of New York at Stony Brook, the researchers compiled nutritional breakdowns of*

---

[11] *American Journal of Clinical Nutrition*, Issue 68, 1998

[12] www.campaignfortruth.com/nutrition.htm

meals offered to patients with no dietary restrictions in 57 university hospitals. Fifty-three of the menus failed to meet all the US Public Health Service's dietary guidelines.'[13]

A colourful account of what might appear on the patient's food tray is included here:

'If you want to know what an average physician thinks about a balanced diet, look at any hospital food fed to patients, doctors, staff and visitors. Iceberg lettuce with a glob of cottage cheese and a wedge of canned pineapple. Slices of overdone and warmed-over beef that have suffered for hours in some electronic purgatory, coated with a gravy made of water, library paste, and bouillon cubes. Peas, corn and carrots, boiled. The pie is a sickening slab of beige goo, flavoured with artificial maple sugar, in a crust of reconstituted cardboard, topped with sweetened shaving cream squirted from an aerosol bomb.'[14]

Dr Andrew Saul comments on western attitudes to diet and nutrition:

'I have seen the foolishness of conventional disease care wisdom. I have seen hospitals feed white bread to patients with bowel cancer and 'Jello' to leukaemia patients. I have seen schools feed bright red 'Slush Puppies' to 7-year-olds for lunch and I have seen children vomit up a desk-top full of red gunk afterwards. And I have seen those same children later line up at the school nursery for hyperactivity drugs.

I have seen hospital patients allowed to go two weeks without a bowel movement. I have seen patients told that they have six months to live when they might live sixty months. I have seen people recover from serious illness, only to have their physician berate them for having used natural healing methods to do so.

---

[13] **Dembling, Sophia**, *Health & Fitness News Service*, http://detnews.com/index.htm, 14th May 1997
[14] 'What supplements don't have': www.mothernature.com

13

I have seen infants spit up formula while their mothers were advised not to breast-feed. I've seen better ingredients in dog food than in the average school or hospital lunch. And I have seen enough.'[15]

Summary

In my books, I examine this problem of doctors in more depth. But for our purposes here, let us firstly appreciate that doctors, while mostly best-intentioned, are working under difficult circumstances in which their treatment options are determined, more often than not, by economic rather than scientific considerations. One key area of their training, namely, the understanding and application of nutritional strategies against disease, has been completely neglected, resulting instead in the patient being given expensive and largely useless chemical remedies with predictable, often serious side-effects. And in among all the technological brouhaha and the testing kits and the whirring machines with their multicoloured cabling and the endless rounds of self-congratulatory conferences in exotic locales around the world discussing the latest in cutting-edge treatments, it isn't so hard to see how the humble glass of water on the conference table was pushed to the back of the blotter out of harm's way.

How the simple truth escaped becoming known.

---

[15] **Saul, Andrew**, *Doctor Yourself* at: www.doctoryourself.com

Water – The Stuff of Life

'Chronic pains of the body which cannot easily be explained as injury or infection, should first and foremost be interpreted as signals of chronic water shortage in the area where the pain is registered. These pain signals should first be considered and excluded as primary indicators for dehydration of the body before any other complicated procedures are forced on the patient.' – Dr F Batmanghelidj

'Insanity: Viewing an overflowing sink and going for the mop instead of the tap.' – Phillip Day

The human body is a bio-electrical water machine that requires a quart a day for every 50 lbs of body weight.[16] The blood alone is made up of a large percentage of watery serum. The lymph fluids which transport waste and nutrients, comprising four times the volume of blood in the body, are made from the water we consume. Every cell that makes us who we are literally owes its life to an adequate supply of fresh, clean water. When the body does not receive a constant, reliable supply of water, it has to ration what is available and cut back on certain functions to make the supply go round. Essential systems like the brain are prioritised, others are impaired or cut back until the brain has decided a reliable source of water has been garnered.

Here's the rub. Most citizens have become chronically and dangerously dehydrated (especially the elderly), since we decided water was too bland to drink and ignored it in favour of tea, coffee, beer, wine, addictive sodas, flavoured water and other chemical-laced water alternatives. A disastrous and dangerous move for the body and society's health in general, to be sure, compounded further since most doctors today cannot readily identify the many water-deficient diseases and associated pains. Thus the underlying dehydration process continues to wreak its havoc while the inevitable drugs given will switch off the warning signals (symptoms).

---

[16] **Batmanghelidj, F**, *Your Body's Many Cries for Water*, Tagman Press, 2000

15

Consider the following conditions:

Heartburn, arthritis, lupus, asthma, 'high cholesterol', high blood pressure, heart disease, cancer formation, hot flushes and menstrual problems, obesity, allergies, bulimia, chronic fatigue syndrome, ME, angina, lower back pain, gout, kidney stones, skin disorders, diabetes, fungal/yeast overgrowths, multiple sclerosis, allergies, migraine headaches, general aches and pains, morning sickness, depression, heavy/burdensome periods, colitis, dyspepsia, peptic ulcers...

All, in various ways, linked to a chronic state of dehydration?

World-renowned water expert Dr Fereydoon Batmanghelidj maintains that the above conditions are the body's many cries for water, complaints dramatically improved with a consistent and long-term intake of fresh, clean water.[17] Dr Batman's best-selling book has helped thousands quash long-term health problems effortlessly and inexpensively. He writes:

'The report of my having successfully treated with water more than three thousand people with symptoms and clinical signs of peptic ulcer disease was published in the Journal of Clinical Gastroenterology in June 1983. I came away from that experience with the understanding that the people I treated were thirsty, and I uncovered the phenomenon that 'pain' in the body indicates thirst, even though the condition is classified as a disease.'[18]

Water is used by the body for digestion, detoxifying cells, watering the lungs, lubricating joints, keeping the body alkalised and a host of cleaning duties. Many warning signals ('symptoms') arise out of the body's inability to neutralise or rid itself of acid, a common enough complaint given the number of antacids sold around the world each day. And the common and dangerous misconception that fuels it?

---

[17] Ibid.
[18] **Batmanghelidj, F**, *Water Cures, Drugs Kill*, Tagman Press, 2003, p. 5

'I drink coffee, tea, diet sodas, beer and a host of other liquids. They contain water, don't they?'

Many of today's designer drinks are diuretic in their effect (water-expelling) because their mostly acidic compositions require the body to give up water in order to eliminate their harmful residues. Diet sodas especially are harmful in that they require large amounts of body-water to neutralise the phosphoric acid component (2.8 pH). Cells that started off healthy and 'plum-like' shrivel to prunes as water, the stuff of life, is progressively denied them. The sick in our hospitals are fed the sodas, tea and coffee they ask for in woeful ignorance of the damage wrought to the micro cell-world within them.

Your body and dehydration
Batmanghelidj's extraordinary work should rightly be considered by a mainstream medical community ever fixated on the drug cure:

- *Brain function*: The brain comprises 2% of the body's total weight, yet receives 15-20% of the blood supply, mostly comprised of water. Dehydration will affect cognitive ability drastically, and, through histamine's action, can create depressive states (many anti-depressant medications are anti-histamines).
- *Bone function*: Bones require plentiful supplies of water. 75% of the weight of the upper body, for instance, is supported by the water core contained within the fifth lumbar disc, the remaining 25% by muscle fibres around the spine.[19]
- *Nerve function*: Microstreams exist along the length of nerves which transport nutrients and conduct energy along microtubules to the synapses to transmit messages. Dehydration disrupts proper nerve function, resulting in the sensation of pain.
- *Hydrolysis*: Water, far from being an inert solvent, is intricately involved in the body's water-dependent chemical reactions. Lack of water means incomplete or

---

[19] Ibid.

faulty metabolic processes, with obvious implications for continued health and well-being. Proteins and enzymes, for instance, do not function as well in acidic solutions of higher viscosity (stickiness) where the body is dehydrated.

- *Cellular energy*: As water is drawn through the cell membrane, its osmotic flow generates a voltage gradient which can be used in the manufacture of ATP and GTP energy. Dehydration will obviously affect the proper functioning of cells and even kill them.

- *Histamine*: This neurotransmitter plays a major role in activating systems which encourage water intake when dehydration is detected. Functions in the body which consume large quantities of water are cut back, namely the bronchial tubes constricted to cut down on water use in the lungs; increased peristalsis in the bowels to wring more water out of faecal material, and so on. Other signs of histamine's activity, namely allergies, asthma, depression and chronic pains, are interpreted by the physician as 'disease' and treated with anti-histamines, pain-killers (analgesics), etc. Thus the signals of thirst are turned off and the dehydration state continues unabated.

- *Dyspepsia (heartburn/reflux)*: Over time, this can lead to ulceration and even cancer. Dr Batmanghelidj recommends that these conditions - also gastritis and duodenitis – be treated with water alone as they are one of the body's major thirst signals. Arrested in his native Iran by the Revolutionary Council during the troubles of the late 1970's, Dr B was confined to Evin prison, Tehran, during which time he successfully treated *with water alone* over three thousand people complaining of dyspeptic pain and associated symptoms.

- *Digestion*: Requires plentiful supplies of water. The stomach relies on mucus lining the walls to shield it from the effects of the stomach's hydrochloric acid. A bicarbonate solution is produced from the cells in the lining which neutralises any acid attempting to break through the mucus. Water is needed to maintain this effective defence system. Too little water, and the mucus barrier is ineffectual, the acid will penetrate and will lead to pain. Ideally, water should be consumed half an hour before a meal, in time to anticipate the production of digestive acid from glands in the stomach wall.

- *Ulcers*: Often located at the valve between the stomach and duodenum. Said to be caused by curved bacteria known as helicobacters. Yet many people have helicobacters in their small intestine, yet not all of them suffer from ulcers. Histamine-producing nerves are located at this site, which monitor the through-put of acidic food chyme from the stomach into the intestine. Histamine has growth-hormone effects on these micro-organisms, resulting in small intestine bacterial overgrowths (SIBOs). Once again, an adequate regime of water intake will allow all the functions relating to digestion to normalise. Prolonged water intake should therefore be considered before more drastic drug treatments are entered into.

Further Resources
Discover the incredible healing powers of water:

Water and Salt, Your Healers from Within
Dr F Batmanghelidj
www.credence.org

(see book review at the back)

Water Under the Bridge

The Damning Case against Fluoridation

'During times of universal deceit, telling the truth becomes a revolutionary act.' - George Orwell

Bringing water to the public is a complicated and responsible business. If you get it wrong, and bacteria afflict the masses, you can definitely lose your pension. Some of the worst scourges mankind has faced have come about as a result of contaminated water supplies, infested with microbes that bring on the feared cholera, dysentery and other fatal syndromes that still afflict most Third World nations today. However, today we like to think problems linked to matters so basic as these are simply gremlins suffered by the less developed nations, not us.

The halogen, chlorine, is often added to the public drinking water to kill germs. When I am in the United States, waiters and waitresses will bring me a glass of iced water, which in many areas is quite undrinkable due to its high chlorine content. Most of the American public has become used to this type of water, and most are prepared to drink it, cook with it, shower with it and wallow around for half an hour in a bath with it with scant regard to the downside. Information on long-term health damage through chlorine exposure is carefully kept from the public, yet most know prolonged chlorine exposure over the years will desiccate the skin, causing premature wrinkling, dandruff and baldness. Concerns over the long-term effects of bad-tasting chlorinated water fuelled a water filter boom in the early 1990s, which is still ongoing. For a few dollars, you can obtain a carbon filter that will screw onto the faucet and strip off the chlorine, delivering what the public believes is clean, uncontaminated H_2O.

But there's another halogen element, which some governments sanction to be put into water supplies, that has caused increasing fear over the past fifty years. Indeed very few public outcries have been as consistent and vigorous as the public's reaction to the fluoridation of water and toothpastes:

'Controversy surrounding the fluoridation experiment has persisted for half a century. Japan and all of continental Europe have rejected the idea for reasons of safety and medical ethics. Experiments in poor countries produced such harmful results that they were quickly halted. Why does fluoridation continue to receive vigorous government and professional backing in the English-speaking nations?' – Health Action Network [20]

Janet Nagel has authored several studies on the subject and explains how the idea of adding fluoride compounds to the water supply gained public support through relentless promotion of this controversial measure by industry and government over sixty years ago:

'In the 1940s and 50s, a vigorous corporate and government promotional campaign convinced large numbers of people that fluorides reduced susceptibility to tooth decay. In 1985, over 90% of all toothpastes sold in the US contained high concentrations of intentionally added fluorine compounds. Close to 60% of the US population consumed water containing 1.0 to 4.0 parts per million of fluoride compounds. Nearly all major US cities, and many smaller ones, intentionally add fluorine compounds to their water supplies.' [21]

So what is 'fluoride' and why exactly is this chemical added to food, water and other products we consume on a daily basis?

The term 'fluoride' is often used to describe fluorine-based chemical additives put into the public water supply or into toothpastes and foods. 'Fluoride' tablets are also prescribed to youngsters apparently to assist in the protection and development of their teeth. In repeatedly hearing the one term, 'fluoride', the public has been cleverly persuaded to imagine there is just one substance that has been made available to us by caring

---

[20] *Fluoridation – Why the Controversy?* Health Action Network briefing document, printed by the National Health Federation, PO Box 688, Monrovia, CA 91017 USA

[21] **Nagel Ed. D, Janet** *Re-examination of Fluoridation Issues*, Health Action Network, op. cit. Statistics are from *Fluoridation Census 1985*, US Public Health Service, Centers for Disease Control (CDC)

government and industry to maintain and promote healthy teeth and gums. The reality is, the term 'fluoride' is used to encompass everything from sodium, calcium and potassium fluorides through to the highly dangerous liquid toxic waste product hexa- (in the US - hydro) -fluorosilicic acid and the toxic powder sodium silicofluoride, both of which are used to fluoridate water supplies.

Pure fluorine is gaseous and is described as 'a non-metallic halogen element that is isolated as a pale yellowish flammable irritating toxic diatomic gas' (Webster's Ninth New Collegiate Dictionary, 1991). Fluorine was used to great effect as a battlefield gas by the militaries during World War 1. Fluoride compounds today are used in pesticides, aluminium smelting, etching metals and glass, aerosol propellants and refrigerants. Sodium fluoride, the same compound that is added to toothpastes under the admiring eye of the world's dental associations, is a chief component of Sarin nerve gas. It's also the main ingredient in rat poison, as any pest control expert will tell you.

The debate surrounding the pros and cons of fluoride additives has raged for half a century. The main areas of contention are as follows:

1) Do fluoride compounds prevent dental caries (cavities) and assist in the development and health maintenance of teeth?
2) Is the fluoridation process merely a convenient way of disposing of heavy industry's toxic wastes?
3) Are fluoride compounds dangerous to public health?
4) Are governments and industry mass-medicating their populations without consent?

Do fluoride compounds reduce dental caries (cavities)?

The belief that fluoride compounds reduce the incidence of tooth decay is dental religion today, in spite of the fact that fluoride's original champion, H Trendley Dean, DDS, admitted under oath almost fifty years ago that his data purporting to prove the efficacy of fluoridation for dental health were not valid.[22]

In June 1993, New Jersey State Assemblyman John V Kelly publicised the disturbing fact that fluoride compounds used in toothpastes and the water supply have never received approval by the American Food & Drug Administration <u>and are officially classified as 'an unapproved new drug'</u>. Kelly's research also uncovered that neither the FDA nor the Institute of Dental Research (NIDR) nor the American Academy of Pediatric Dentistry could furnish any proof of fluoride compound safety or effectiveness as required by law as part of the FDA drug approval process. Which means of course that in the US, almost every American is receiving treatment every day from a drug which is unapproved by the FDA.[23] This in turn means that doctors and dentists prescribing fluoride compounds to patients are committing an illegal act and that the fluoridation of public water supplies is medical experimentation without the target population's consent. If fluoride compounds are, as their proponents exhort, the greatest things to hit the teeth of humanity since dentists (another debatable point), then why hasn't the FDA approved these 'valuable' compounds? We'll find out as we proceed.

The Grand Rapids fluoride trials

One of the first trials carried out in an attempt to prove fluoridation's effectiveness in reducing dental decay occurred in America in 1945 and involved the cities of Grand Rapids and Muskegon, Michigan. Grand Rapids' public water supply was fluoridated and Muskegon's was left alone to serve as the control. Within a couple of years, pro-fluoride advocates were clamouring that fluoridation was producing a 60% drop in dental caries in Grand Rapids when compared with those occurring in the city of Muskegon. The results were apparently so conclusive that this ten-year trial was halted after just five years whereupon the authorities fluoridated Muskegon's water supplies.

---

[22] *City of Oroville vs. Public Utilities Commission of the State of California* – H Trendley Dean Proceedings, Oroville, California, 20th –21st October 1955

[23] Trenton *Star Ledger*, 'Kelly Seeks FDA Ban on Fluoride Supplement' by Guy Sterling, 4th July 1993; also Letter to US FDA Commissioner David Kessler by John V Kelly, 3rd June 1993

Later however, the results of the trials were to reveal disturbing inconsistencies in the collection and reporting of the data. One graph shows that within one year, dental decay had declined 70.5% among six-year-olds in Grand Rapids, when studies were made of all 79 schools in the trial area. The reality is that the data used to start the trial included dental decay rates for all 79 schools, but from 1946 onwards, only the children from 25 hand-selected schools in the trial area were examined, giving rise to an apparent drop in decay rates. During the next three years, the dental decay rates actually rose by 65.2% among the 25 schools, indicating that fluoridation was having no effect in spite of the children (selectively chosen) having the apparent benefit of more years of fluoridation.[24] The only 'reduction' in decay rates had occurred during the year of the selection process.

The Kingston/Newburgh trial

A similar US study was conducted with the cities of Kingston and Newburgh, located in New York State along the Hudson River. Newburgh was to be the fluoridated township and Kingston the unfluoridated control. Within ten years of the study inception in 1945, Public Health fluoridation supporters were claiming a 60% decline in dental decay occurring in Newburgh. Not revealed however was the fact that Newburgh parents and their children received free consultations on dental hygiene, advice on the boycotting of sweets and dental visits to remove dental plaque. Someone somewhere wanted Newburgh to succeed. Kingston however was completely ignored and received no such advantages. Later it became apparent that not all the Newburgh children had been selected. Another bout of selective reporting had occurred.

After announcing their victory with fluoridation however, the Public Health Service proponents of fluoridation received a major slap in the face. For, during the tenth year of Newburgh's fluoridation, an independent study of the two townships had been underway, carried out by Dr John A Forst, Professor at the University of the State of New York and chief of the State Bureau

---

24 *National Research Council*, publication #214

of Health Services. He too studied both sets of school children and his results painted a disturbingly different picture:

	Kingston	Newburgh
Enrolled	5403	5119
Pupils Inspected	5303 (98%)	4959 (97%)
Pupils with Dental Defects	2209 (41.6%)	3139 (63.2%)
Pupils under Dental Treatment	1551 (29.2%)	2072 (41.7%)

These shocking results were too clear to be ignored. After ten years of fluoridation and when nearly all the children of both townships were examined, it was evident that Newburgh contained more children with dental defects and more children undergoing dental treatment than in Kingston, a township left to its own water devices. To this day, Kingston remains unfluoridated, having vigorously rejected fluoridation at the conclusion of the trials. Later, a follow-up study in 1989 would show that after almost four decades of fluoridation, schoolchildren in Newburgh had no less dental decay than in unfluoridated Kingston.[25]

Research by the UK's Safe Water Society yielded similar research results:

1) A US trial studying 50,000 inhabitants across 68 US cities in 1986-7 showed that fluoride increased tooth decay.[26]
2) 400,000 children were studied in India and calcium and fluoride levels were measured. The study found that fluoride increases tooth decay while calcium reduces caries.[27]
3) 21,000 Japanese children were studied in 1972. Fluoride was found to increase tooth decay.[28]
4) After 20 years of water fluoridation in Seattle, Washington State, authorities reported an unprecedented dental crisis in the north-western American city.[29]

[25] **Kumar JV, et al** *American Journal of Public Health*, 1989; 79:565-569
[26] **Yiamouyiannis, J** *Fluoride 23 #2*, April 1990
[27] **Teotia, SP** *Fluoride*, April 1994 pp.59-66
[28] **Imai, Y** *Japanese Journal of Dental Health*, 1972; 22:144-196
[29] **Porterfield, Elaine** *Tacoma Morning News Tribune*, 'Demand Taxes Clinics Serving the

5) 22,000 children were studied in Tucson, Arizona. Fluoride was found to increase tooth decay.[30]
6) In 1987, Alan S Gray, DDS, FRCD(C), Director of the Division of Dental Health Services or the British Columbia Ministry of Health, called for a re-examination of the relevance of fluoride compounds in the Canadian public water supply when it was learned that tooth decay rates in British Columbia (where only 11% of the population use fluoridated water) were lower than those of other Canadian provinces with fluoridation rates of 40%-70%.[31]
7) In December 1993, a Canadian Dental Association committee, known as the Canadian Workshop on the Evaluation of Current Recommendations Concerning Fluorides, concluded that consuming fluoride does not prevent tooth decay or reduce its incidence. The panel also found that children exposed to fluoride compounds risked dental fluorosis.[32]

Leading fluoridation opponent John R Lee MD reports that doctors and researchers are often in for a bumpy ride if they question fluoride's efficacy and challenge its alleged safety and cost-effectiveness:

'When one looks in the dental literature for evidence that fluoridation reduces dental costs, the results are equally dismal. In all studies in which selection bias is not evident [i.e. where the data hasn't been fudged], *no reduction in dental costs is found. When Dr Gray, a dental health officer in Vancouver, BC, Canada, examined* [the records of] *all schoolchildren in British Columbia, he found no dental benefit from fluoridation. Upon reporting this, he was demoted and obliged to desist in making any comment about it.'*[33]

Poor', 30th March 1992

[30] **Cornelius Steelinck** *Chemical and Engineering News,* 27th January 1992, p.2; also *Science News,* 5th March 1994, p.159

[31] **Gray, A S** *Journal of the Canadian Dental Association,* 'Fluoridation – Time for New Baseline?' October 1987

[32] **Clark, Christopher** *Canadian Medical Association Journal,* 1993:149 (12), 15th December 1993

[33] **Lee, John R** *Fluoridation Follies,* a research paper, September 1995, p.13

Delivering the target dose of 1.0mg fluoride compounds to each citizen every day costs money – and for what benefit, against what risk? Even supposing one believes in the efficacy of fluorides for dental health against all reason and scientific evidence, why fluoridate the water supply? Why not just pass out the tablets? In other words, *why deliberately spend more*? According to one public water supply co-ordinator, the annual projected budget for fluoridating the water supply of Tacoma, Washington State was estimated to be $125,000 in 1991.[34] The cost of supplying fluoride tablets to the under 12s would be a mere $1.20 per thousand 1.0 mg tablets in comparison. Which naturally begs the question: *Why the fixation on medicating the water supplies?*

Fluoridation – Disposal of heavy industry's toxic wastes

During the first four decades of the 1900s, global industrial output rose dramatically. During two world wars, industry increased production many orders of magnitude in order to satisfy the demand for munitions, armaments, tanks and aircraft. Agriculture too was honed to a knife-edge. All available hands were put to the land in order to ensure the continuance of food output to beleaguered nations.

Both heavy manufacturing and the agro-chemical industries produce large quantities of fluoride compounds as toxic waste products. During the course of these activities, as early as the 1930s, fluoride in industrial emissions was increasingly regarded as a major pollutant. After the war, the major industrial nations began exporting fertilisers and heavy industrial goods to lesser-developed countries resulting in their gross national output expanding exponentially. By 1965, President Lyndon Johnson's Science Advisory Committee was naming fluoride compounds as one of America's four leading pollutants.[35]

---

[34] **Myrick, C R** Water Quality Co-Ordinator, City of Tacoma, in a telephone conversation with Wini Silko, Tacoma citizen, 15th November, 1991 (Health Action Network briefing document)

[35] **Jerard, Elise** 'Total Fluoride Exposure', a report prepared for the Municipal Broadcasting System, September 1968

Ironically, since water fluoridation was proposed in the 1940s, very little has been heard from the establishment regarding fluoride as an environmental pollutant. Clearly, the chemical and heavy manufacturing industries had a growing problem on their hands with raw toxic fluoride wastes, which also contained many metals harmful to human and animal health, such as cadmium, beryllium, lead, mercury and aluminium. Industry, faced with millions of dollars in operating costs to dispose of toxic waste in an acceptable manner, found themselves considering ways in which the problem could be dissolved, a little at a time, with little or no cost to their margins. Janet Nagel remarks:

'Laws controlling the disposal of toxic wastes do not permit the industries creating these fluorides to release them into the environment. However, the 'laundering' process of fluoridation allows these same toxins to be spread indiscriminately on lawns and gardens, incorporated into processed foods, and released by the ton into water and air, in sewer effluent and sludge.

The original promotion of fluoridation as a remedy for tooth decay was funded by the aluminum [sic] industry. Andrew Mellon, former Chairman of the Aluminum Corporation of America (ALCOA), was Secretary of the Treasury when the US Public Health Service was an agency of the Treasury Department. The research purporting to demonstrate fluoride effectiveness and safety was funded by ALCOA, Reynolds Metals, and other heavy fluoride emitters.'[36]

No worries

Government and industry have long denied that fluoride additives are toxic waste from industry, preferring to paint a picture of sanitised, benevolent chemicals guarding our teeth day and night administered through the 'safe' water we drink. The reality is, even those within government ranks have broken cover and confirmed the source of these chemicals. Tom Reeves, for example, a water engineer with America's Centers for Disease

---

[36] Nagel, Janet, op. cit; also Griffiths, Joel, op. cit.

Control (CDC), controversially admitted in January 2001 that fluoride additives were waste emissions from heavy industry:

'All of the fluoride chemicals used in the U.S. for water fluoridation - sodium fluoride, sodium fluorosilicate, and fluorosilicic acid - are by-products of the phosphate fertilizer industry.

The manufacturing process produces two by-products: (1) a solid, calcium sulphate (sheetrock, CaSo₄); and (2) the gases, hydrofluoric acid (HF) and silicon tetrafluoride (SiF₄). A simplified explanation of this manufacturing process follows: Apatite rock, a calcium mineral found in central Florida, is ground up and treated with sulfuric acid, producing phosphoric acid and the two by-products, calcium sulphate and the two gas emissions. Those gases are captured by product recovery units (scrubbers) and condensed into 23% fluorosilicic acid (H_2SiF_6). Sodium fluoride and sodium fluorosilicate are made from this acid.'

Are fluoride compounds dangerous to public health?

Undeniably, fluorides used in the drinking water supplies are a toxic, non-biodegradable, environmental pollutant, officially classified as a contaminant by the US Environmental Protection Agency. Hexafluorosilicic acid, the most commonly used fluoridation additive, contains other toxic substances which can include lead, beryllium, mercury, cadmium and arsenic.[37] Sodium fluoride, beloved of toothpaste manufacturers, is a hazardous waste compound from the aluminium smelting process, and is also used in water fluoridation schemes, although less frequently than the previously mentioned two compounds. Sodium fluoride is often given to children in tablet or liquid form and is almost always added to toothpastes in concentrations of between 500-1500 ppm.

Interestingly, Proctor and Gamble, the manufacturers of Crest toothpaste and, predictably, ardent supporters of sodium fluoride, were reported to have admitted that a family size tube of their

---

37 **d'Raye, Tonita**, *The Facts About Fluoride*, PO Box 21075, Keizer, OR 97307 USA

world famous toothpaste contained enough sodium fluoride to kill a 20-30lb child if ingested.[38] Warning labels appear on American toothpaste packaging advising that in the event of ingestion, the victim should seek a poisons control centre immediately. This notice is made the more ridiculous when one considers you don't have to swallow poisons for them to become absorbed, *if they're under the tongue, they're in the bloodstream.*

This author has met several elderly gentlemen in the UK who recalled one way conscripts used to attempt to dodge the National Service draft in the 1950s. They would consume half a tube of toothpaste, which subsequently made the recruit extremely ill and unfit to serve.

US federal research found fluoride caused cancer in humans and animals.[39] The National Cancer Institute's Dr Dean Burk was constrained to state: *'It is concluded that artificial fluoridation appears to cause or induce about 20-30 excess cancer deaths for every 100,000 persons exposed per year after about 15-20 years.'*[40] As far back as October 1944, the *Journal of the American Medical Association* published an editorial stating: *'... that the use of drinking water containing as little as 1.2 to 3 parts per million of fluoride will cause such developmental disturbances in bones as osteosclerosis, spondylosis, and osteoporosis, as well as goitre.'*[41] The Safe Water Foundation filed US Freedom on Information Act requests to obtain the results of government studies. Dr John Yiamouyiannis (president of the Safe Water Foundation) said, after studying the information, *'All tests came out positive'*, establishing a fluoride-cancer link.[42]

Yet, in spite of all, incredibly to this day not only is fluoridation still permitted, US federal goals as well as targets in Australia,

---

[38] *Spotlight*, 28th October 1996, p.8

[39] National Toxicology Program (NTP) 1990, National Cancer Institute, HHS Fluoride Report 2/91

[40] www.thewinds.org/archive/medical/fluoride01-98.html

[41] *Journal of the American Medical Association*, 'Health Damaging Effects of Fluoride', October 1944

[42] www.whale.to/Dental/fluoride.html

New Zealand and the UK strive for mandatory fluoridation of national water supplies at the earliest opportunity.

Fluoride safe?
You be the judge!

> Fluoride accumulates in the body like lead, inflicting its damage over long periods of time. Fluoride is more toxic than lead, and slightly less toxic than arsenic. Lead is given a toxicity rating of 3, whereas fluoride's level is 4. Under US law, administered and enforced by the Environmental Protection Agency, the maximum allowable lead in drinking water is 0.015mg/litre. With fluoride however it is 4.0mg/litre, OVER 350 TIMES THE PERMITTED LEAD LEVEL. [43]

> Fluoride compounds initially cause dental fluorosis, a chalky mottling of the tooth enamel, leading to brittle and vulnerable teeth. Fluorosis is a permanent malformation of tooth enamel indicating an alteration in bone growth. Further symptoms of chronic fluoride poisoning may include constipation, excess gas and other gastrointestinal disturbances, chronic boils or rashes, peeling, shrivelled skin between your toes or brittle, easy-to-break nails. Symptoms of extreme fluoride poisoning may include chronic fatigue syndrome, skin problems, bleeding gums, excess saliva, hair loss, edema swelling in the lower extremities, mental problems, kidney disease, cancer and death. [44]

> *'The fluoride dose prescribed by doctors and the dose administered without prescription to everyone in community drinking water is EXPECTED to cause dental fluorosis in 10% of children. Actual Public Health Service figures show that 30% of children in fluoridated localities have dental fluorosis, and 10% of children in*

---

43 *Clinical Toxicology of Commercial Products*, 5th Ed. 1984

44 Dr Leo Spira's testimony before a US Senate investigative committee explained that the long-term effects of fluoride compound poisoning potentially implicated the chemical in a host of problems not readily identifiable as fluoride-causation, in view of the length of exposure.

non-fluoridated areas now have fluorosis.'[45] Even citizens living in non-fluoridated areas are expected to ingest amounts in excess of 1.0mg fluoride compounds per day through toothpaste use and consumption of food products manufactured with fluoridated water. Citizens living in fluoridated communities <u>may expect to be exposed to 5.0mg a day or more.</u>

➢ Medical research shows that hip fractures are 20-40% higher in fluoridated communities. [46]

➢ Fluorides are used in laboratory work to inhibit enzyme activity. Fluoride compounds have the same effect in the human body, accumulating in the skeleton structure over long periods of time. Fluoride poisoning is long-term and progressive.

➢ The chemicals injected into public water supplies to elevate fluoride levels are raw industrial waste. The two most commonly used additives are hexafluorosilicic acid and sodium silicofluoride, toxic by-products of aluminium smelting and phosphate fertiliser production.

➢ Fluoridated water increases corrosion and leaching of lead from water mains and plumbing.

➢ About 1% of the fluoridated water used from public supplies is actually ingested by the public. The remainder is used for sewage, washing, industry and agriculture. This had led to the belief by industry that fluoridated industrial waste may be safely disposed of in this manner with little or no harm to the public. However, fluoride levels in the sewer effluent of fluoridated water systems are not monitored or controlled. Fish have been found to be poisoned by fluoride emissions at and below the 'acceptable' levels emitted by sewer effluent.[47]

---

45 *Health Action Network* briefing document, op. cit. Also, *Review of Fluoride Benefits and Risks*, US Public Health Service, February 1991, p.53
46 *The John R Lee MD Medical Letter*, February 1999
47 Health Action Network, op. cit.

Fluoridation -
Mass-medication without consent?

Water fluoridation has been described as the widest mass-medication program in the history of humanity. That this procedure is occurring without the informed consent of the citizenry is the chief ethical issue that has driven opposition to fluoridation since World War 2. Researcher Janet Nagel summarises:

'That nearly all physicians, dentists and other members of the dominant health professions have come to hold such uncritical faith in fluoride as a tooth decay remedy raises serious questions about the content and quality of their training as scientists and practitioners. That so many professional leaders and government officials have been willing to falsify or obscure scientific data in their zeal to maintain the fluoridation pretense raises concerns that are even more far-reaching.' [48]

The charge of mass medication of the population can justifiably be made since fluoride is, by the admission of its proponents, pharmacologically active in supposedly preventing dental caries. Many of the trials quoted in this chapter demonstrate quite inarguably that fluoride compounds are also pharmacologically active in doing human and animal systems harm. Even the Food & Drug Administration wishes the whole fluoride embarrassment would go away, having classified water fluoride compounds as 'unapproved new drugs' and obstinately left it at that. On the 16th March 1979, a surreptitious changing of the Federal Register occurred on page 16006. All paragraphs stating that fluoride compounds were 'essential or probably essential' were deleted by the FDA.

There are not many who will dispute the fact that fluoride compounds in amounts of 1.0 ppm (as advocated by fluoride proponents) do not produce changes in tooth enamel structure and bone formation. The point being made by fluoride opponents is that the citizens themselves should have the right to decide

---

[48] Ibid.

whether or not to take fluoride supplementation. At the present time, there is no regulation as to how much fluoride any given individual is taking in, due to varied water consumption, age, occupation, diet and lifestyle. This has led to obvious concerns over health risks which have failed to disperse over the last fifty years, which only serve to underline more forcibly the unassailable conclusion that there are no known essential uses for fluoride compounds in medicine or dentistry.

As one last example of how even experts in the field of chemistry and medicine have remained divided on this issue over the years, the following Nobel Prize winners have either expressed reservations about fluoridation, or have outright opposed it. They are:

Adolf Butenandt (Chemistry, 1939)
Arvid Carlsson (Chemistry, 2000)
Hans von Euler-Chelpin (Chemistry, 1929)
Walter Rudolf Hess (Medicine, 1949)
Corneille Jean-François Heymans (Medicine, 1938)
Sir Cyril Norman Hinshelwood (Chemistry, 1956)
Joshua Lederberg (Medicine, 1958)
William P. Murphy (Medicine, 1934)
Giulio Natta (Chemistry 1963)
Sir Robert Robinson (Chemistry, 1947)
Nikolai Semenov (Chemistry, 1956)
James B. Sumner (Chemistry, 1946)
 Hugo Theorell (Medicine, 1955)
Artturi Virtanen (Chemistry, 1945)[49]

Notepad
Dr John Lee summarises:

FACT 1
Fluoridation is cancer-causing, cancer-promoting, and is linked to increased cancer rates in humans.[50]

---

49 The Fluoridation Action Network, www.fluoridealert.org
50 *Carcinogenesis*, Vol. 9, 1988 pp.2279-2284; 'Sodium Fluoride; Individual Animal Tumor

FACT 2

Hip fracture rates are substantially higher in people residing in fluoridated communities.[51]

FACT 3

Dental fluorosis, the first visible sign of fluoride poisoning, affects from 8% to 51% of the children drinking fluoridated water.[52]

FACT 4

All of the recent large-scale studies on fluoridation and tooth decay show that fluoridation does not reduce tooth decay.[53]

FACT 5

Fluoride drops and tablets are not approved by the US Food & Drug Administration as safe and effective. On the contrary, fluoride tablets and drops have been shown to be ineffective in reducing tooth decay and can cause skin eruptions, gastric distress, headache and weakness, which disappear when fluoride use is discontinued. Dental fluorosis on the other hand, is a permanent disfigurement.[54]

For more information on fluoride issues
www.fluoridealert.org

Pathology Table [rats], Battelle Memorial Institute, 23rd February 1989; *Lancet* 36 1990, p.737; *Review of Fluoride: Benefits and Risks*, US Public Health Service, 1991, pp. F1-F7; *Fluoride*, Vol. 26, 1992, pp.83-96; *A Brief Report on the Association of Drinking Water Fluoridation and the Incidence of Osteosarcoma Among Young Males*, New Jersey Department of Health, November 1992; *Fluoride, the Aging Factor*, Health Action Press, 1993, pp.72-90

[51] *Journal of the American Medical Association (JAMA)*, Vol. 264, 1990, pp.500-502; *JAMA*, Vol. 266, 1991, pp.513-514; *JAMA*, Vol. 268, 1992, pp.746-748; *JAMA*, Vol. 273, 1995, pp. 775-776

[52] *Science*, Vol. 217, 1982, pp.26-30; *Journal of the American Dental Association*, Vol. 108, 1984, pp.56-59; *Journal of Public Health Dentistry*, Vol. 46, 1986, pp.184-187; *Health Effects of Ingested Fluoride*, National Research Council, 1993, p.37

[53] *Community Health Studies*, Vol. 11, 1987, pp.85-90; *Journal of the Canadian Dental Association*, Vol. 53, 1987, pp.763-765; *Fluoride*, Vol. 23, 1990, pp.55-67

[54] Letter from Frank R Fazzari, Chief, Prescription Drug Compliance, US Food & Drug Administration to New Jersey Assemblyman John Kelly, 8th June 1993; *Preventing Tooth Decay: Results from a Four-Year National Study*, Robert Wood-Johnson Foundation, Special Report #2/1983, 18 pages; *Community Dentistry and Oral Epidemiology*, Vol. 19, 1991, pp.88-92; *1992 Physicians Desk Reference*, p.2273

So, Which Water?

There is a lot of snobbery about water. Commercial rivalries rear their heads as the Western world gradually awakens to the reality of medicated, polluted water and the need to do something about it. The water boards insist their water is safe (why wouldn't they?), and write off such 'scaremongering' as a ploy to create problems to sell water filters. Some of these are the same water boards tipping industrial poisons into the water supply and convincing themselves they are doing the public a service. Such is life.

Water contaminants

Below are list of the more common contaminants found in water supplies all over the western world.

Chlorine	Arsenic
Fluoride	Radium
Trihalomethanes	Aluminium
Nitrates	Copper
Hormones (and medications)	Lead
Petrol and MTBE	Mercury
Bacteria, viruses and	Cadmium
Other micro-organisms	Barium

One point often missed is the non-ionised mineralisation of the water which the body finds hard to assimilate. Much of this will be sludge the body has to deal with along with the rest of the pollutants. A simple electrolysis test of the water will precipitate soluents out of solution so they will be visible. While the ugly mass resulting is sometimes misinterpreted as 'all pollution', there is an ionised mineral content which the body is able to use. The problem though has been to separate any useable mineral content from the rest of the junk.

While it is true to state that most tap water is 'fresher' than its bottled water counterpart, tap water is nevertheless recycled and often pollutants are not taken out. Years of birth control pills and endless prescriptions for Prozac, Paxil, etc. end up down the toilet in the urine and faeces and these hormones and drugs are often detectable in water supplies *after* the water is supposed to have been treated. It has long been untrue that drinking tap water is 'safe' over the long haul, and even more so if your supplies have been fluoridated or chlorinated.[55]

Filtration solutions

It is my belief that not too many years from now, the world will see houses built with in-house filtration systems as standard. Point-of-use (POU) filtration is the most reliable way to ensure the quality and freshness of the water you are drinking. Let's take a quick look at water supply alternatives.

Supermarket (bottled) water

...contains reasonably high mineral content (250-400 ppm), a lot of which the body is not able to use (non-ionised). This water has sat around for a while and often is not as fresh as the providers would have you believe. Also, several recent scandals have highlighted that, far from being the 'spring water' advertised, the bottling company merely took the neighbourhood water supply and ran it through a carbon filter before filling the bottles and slapping on the scenic labels. Avoid plastic bottles, especially the flexible ones, which contain plasticiser chemicals which mimic the female hormone estrogen. Glass bottles, while awkward, do not give off this problem. Bottled water is inconveniently expensive, and you end up with arms like an orang-utan after all those trips to the corner-store.

Carbon filtration

These filters are inexpensive and available from your neighbourhood DIY store. The common ones are either stand-alone units (you pour the water in at the top, and the cleaner stuff comes out at the bottom), or counter-top units which attach to the tap/faucet in the kitchen and filter the water as it passes through. Carbon filters are good at removing most of the chlorine in

---

[55] The Fluoridation Action Network, op. cit.

countries like America and Canada where the water is heavily polluted with this halogen. You end up with tastier water, but any fluorides, heavy metals, hormones and micro-organisms remain untouched.

Distillation

The nectar of many health gurus. Lots of problems, I'm afraid. In distillation, the water is boiled, evaporated, then the vapour condensed, thus removing all soluents and leaving pure water. Sounds too good to be true, right? It is. Dr Joseph Mercola explains:

'Distilled water is free of dissolved minerals and, because of this, has the special property of being able actively to absorb toxic substances from the body and eliminate them. Studies validate the benefits of drinking distilled water when one is seeking to cleanse or detoxify the system for short periods of time (a few weeks at a time).

Fasting using distilled water can be dangerous because of the rapid loss of electrolytes (sodium, potassium, chloride) and trace minerals like magnesium, deficiencies of which can cause heart beat irregularities and high blood pressure. Cooking foods in distilled water pulls the minerals out of them and lowers their nutrient value.

Distilled water is an active absorber and when it comes into contact with air, it absorbs carbon dioxide, making it acidic. The more distilled water a person drinks, the higher the body acidity becomes.

The most toxic commercial beverages that people consume (i.e. cola beverages and other soft drinks) are made from distilled water. Studies have consistently shown that heavy consumers of soft drinks (with or without sugar) spill huge amounts of calcium, magnesium and other trace minerals into the urine.

Not good, then. According to the U.S. Environmental Protection Agency, *'Distilled water, being essentially mineral-free, is very aggressive, in that it tends to dissolve substances with which it is in contact. Notably, carbon dioxide from the air is rapidly absorbed, making the water acidic and even more aggressive. Many metals are dissolved by distilled water.'*

Reverse osmosis filtration (RO)

... is my filtration system of choice. First pioneered by the French in 1748, RO is used today for manned space programs, desalination of sea water as well as use in heavy industry where the purest, most stable water is required.

How RO works

The RO membrane is extremely fine and selective about what it allows through. Water, due to its small molecular size, passes through easily, while soluent contaminants become trapped. Water will typically be present on both sides of the membrane, with each side having a different concentration of dissolved minerals. On the *Science – How Stuff Works* web-site, we read:

'Since the water in the less concentrated solution seeks to dilute the more concentrated solution, water will pass through the membrane from the lower concentration side to the greater concentration side. Eventually, osmotic pressure will counter the diffusion process exactly, and an equilibrium will form.

The process of reverse osmosis forces water with a greater concentration of contaminants (the source water) into a tank containing water with an extremely low concentration of contaminants (the processed water). High water pressure on the source side is used to 'reverse' the natural osmotic process, with the semi-permeable membrane still permitting the passage of water while rejecting most of the other contaminants. The specific process through which this occurs is called ion exclusion, in which a concentration of ions at the membrane surface from a barrier that allows other water molecules to pass through while excluding other substances.'

What does RO remove?

Reverse osmosis is used to remove a cross-section of health and aesthetic contaminants: Chlorine, fluorides, hormones, micro-organisms such as viruses and bacteria, heavy metals, and heavy industrial 'volatile' contaminants, such as benzene, trichloroethylene, trihalomethanes and radon. The Water Quality Association (WQA) cautions however that while RO membranes typically remove virtually all known micro-organisms and most other health contaminants, design considerations may prevent a unit from offering foolproof protection when incorporated into a consumer drinking water system. Always ensure the unit you buy has been tested successfully and approved by a quality testing laboratory.

What's in an RO system?

A reverse osmosis system for the house typically comprises:

- A low pressure storage tank
- Carbon and sediment pre-filtration units
- The reverse osmosis semi-permeable membrane
- Odour and taste control post carbon filter
- Connecting pipes and miscellaneous kit
- Instructions

The *Water Review Technical Brief* explains: *'Low pressure units typically provide between 24 and 35 gallons per day of water. Water purity can be as high as 95 percent of rejection. These systems can be highly affordable, under-sink units starting at about £699.00. These units produce water for a cost as low as five cents per gallon once maintenance and water costs are factored in. Maintenance usually requires replacing any pre- or postfilters (typically one to four times per year); and the reverse osmosis cartridge once every two to three years, depending on usage.'*

Pura-Flow Reverse Osmosis

Thankfully, since that article was published, the price of good reverse osmosis systems has come down considerably, making the process affordable and desirable for every household. Credence has investigated many filtration systems and now markets the highly advanced *Pura-Flow* unit that meets our exacting standards.

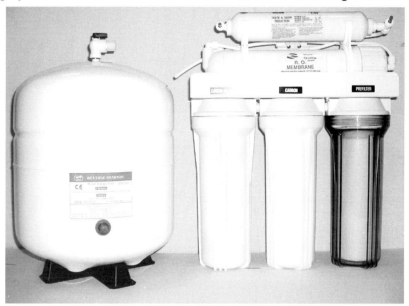

I give this product my hearty endorsement, not only because of its superb reliability and performance, but also because it retails for up to half the cost of more expensive and less efficient models. With operating costs factored in over a five-year period (filter changes, etc.), RO water may be produced by *Pura-Flow* for as little as a couple of pence per gallon. Quite an improvement over the supermarket stuff, without all the lugging and the monkey arms!

Can I fit *Pura-Flow* myself?

Those with average DIY smarts should have no problem if they follow the instructions. Those who prefer someone else to do the work may call upon a local plumber to install. Filter changes are straightforward to carry out. The pre-carbon/sludge filters are changed the most regularly (every six months) while the RO membrane and odour and taste control cartridge last far longer. A TDS meter (total dissolved solids measuring device) is included with the kit, along with the instructions, so water may be periodically tested for purity, and notification learned of any degradation of the filters.

Conclusion

There is no more important substance for good health than water. Your body cries out for it, your blood is made up of it, nerves, heart, lungs, bowels and brain do not function without it, yet we answer the body's thirst signals with tea, coffee, Fanta, Diet Coke, Budweiser and drugs! Hardly any wonder most western nations have a pub/bar culture to deal with the ravening thirst of their citizens.

Many illnesses respond well to adequate hydration, according to the experts. Mental performance is enhanced. Limbs operate. Blood thinned. Pain banished. Bowels happy. Skin lustrous and clear. Toxins flushed away. Water, the stuff for life.

Are you getting enough of it?

May I finish by wholeheartedly recommending every thirst-wracked body read Dr Batmanghelidj's masterful *Water and Salt* book (see overleaf). Dr Batman is right to anticipate his glorious findings will open the sluice gates of a new understanding in medical science. Which, if one pauses to ponder, might be the ultimate irony.

Two atoms of hydrogen, and one of oxygen.

Set to flood the world with its substance.

Again.

Water and Salt
Your Healers from Within

By Dr F Batmanghelidj (194 pages)
Tagman Press, 2003

It needs no prescription. It is freely available. It costs nothing. It has no dangerous side-effects. It is the medication your body cries for when it is stressed. It is good old plain, natural water...

The world-famous expert on water, Dr F Batmanghelidj, draws together nearly 25 years of research on the amazing healing properties of water, as well as exploding the modern health myth that salt is bad for us. He applies his findings to a wide range of ailments, including heart disease, allergies, asthma, osteoporosis, sleep disorders, depression, addiction, infection, diabetes, menopausal problems, arthritis, auto-immune diseases and obesity.

Don't miss this!
Available from www.credence.org
Or see **Contacts! Contacts! Contacts!**

Contacts! Contacts! Contacts!

If you wish to purchase more copies of this book or order a
Pura-Flow Reverse Osmosis System, please use the contact
details below.

> **Vital Minerals**
> **UK Orders:** (01622) 832386
> **Int'l Orders:** +44 1622 832386
> **UK Fax:** (01622) 833314
> **www.vitalminerals.org**

Obtaining product information

If you need more information, a list of other health-giving
Credence titles, or help on any of the materials discussed in
this book, please use the contact details below:

Credence
PO Box 3
TONBRIDGE
Kent TN12 9ZY
England
info@credence.org

About the Author

Phillip Day was born in England in 1960. He was educated at the British education establishments Selwyn and Charterhouse, and throughout his twenties had a successful entrepreneurial career founding businesses in sales and marketing. With a firm grounding in business and the ways of the media, Phillip's research career began after he became interested in wars going on in health and politics over issues that were being deliberately withheld or misreported to the public.

Phillip Day heads up the publishing and research organisation Credence, which collates the work provided by researchers in many fields. He is also founder of the world-wide Campaign for Truth in Medicine (CTM), whose free monthly Internet newsletter may be obtained by registering at www.campaignfortruth.com. CTM's intention is to work with the establishments and organisations concerned to resolve health issues that are harmful to the public, and to provide the necessary information for citizens to make their own informed choices in these vital matters. Phillip's speaking schedule is exhaustive and takes him to audiences all over the world.

He is married to Samantha and lives in Kent, England.

Books by Phillip Day: *Cancer: Why We're Still Dying to Know the Truth, Health Wars, The Mind Game, The ABC's of Disease, Ten Minutes to Midnight, Food For Thought, B17 Metabolic Therapy, Colonics, World Without AIDS, Water: Stuff of Life.*